SWANSON

EASY
LOW·FAT
RECIPES
WITH SWANSON BROTH

Swanson Broth's *Easy Low-Fat Recipes* was produced by the Global Publishing division of Campbell Soup Company, Campbell Place, Camden, NJ 08103-1799.

Senior Managing Editor:	Pat Teberg
Assistant Editors:	Peg Romano, Ginny Gance, Joanne Fullan
Marketing Managers:	Kathryn Block, Mike Senackerib
Public Relations Manager:	Mary Beth Kramer
Promotions Manager:	Marion Williams
Director, Global Design Center:	William Lunderman
Global Consumer Food Center:	Jane Freiman, Peggy Apice, Nancy Speth, Sue Lawrence
Nutrition Science:	Carole Dichter, D.Sc., R.D.; Patricia Locket, M.S., R.D.
Photography:	Stephen Hone, Stephen Hone Studio/Philadelphia
Photo Stylists/Production:	Clare Hone, Ruth Bowen, Jackie Neale
Food Stylists:	Debbie Wahl, assisted by Nancy McClunin, Peg Romano

Designed and published by Meredith Custom Publishing, 1912 Grand Avenue, Des Moines, IA 50309-3379. Printed in Hong Kong.

Pictured on the front cover: *Citrus Skillet Chicken and Rice* (page 54).

Preparation and Cooking Times: Every recipe was developed and tested in Campbell's Global Consumer Food Center by professional home economists. Use "Chill Time," "Cook Time," "Prep Time," "Marinating Time" and/or "Stand Time" given with each recipe as guides. The preparation times are based on the approximate amount of time required to assemble the recipes *before* baking or cooking. These times include preparation steps, such as chopping; mixing; cooking rice, pasta, vegetables; etc. The fact that some preparation steps can be done simultaneously or during cooking is taken into account. The cook times are based on the minimum amount of time required to cook, bake or broil the food in the recipes.

Recipe and Nutrition Values: Values are approximate; calculations are based upon food composition data in the Campbell Soup Company Master Data Base. Some variation in nutrition values may result from periodic product changes.

Calculation of Nutritional Information: Optional ingredients are omitted. When a choice is given for an ingredient, calculations are based upon the first choice listed. Garnishes and "if desired" ingredients are not included in the calculations. The following information is provided for each recipe serving: calories; total fat; saturated fat; total carbohydrate and protein in grams (g); and cholesterol and sodium in milligrams (mg).

For sending us glassware, flatware, dinnerware and serving accessories, a special thanks to: *Bernardaud New York, Inc.*, New York, NY on pages 4-5, 17, 19, 48-49 and 57; *Christofle*, New York, NY on pages 23, 27 and 71; *Fitz and Floyd*, Dallas, TX on pages 9, 21, 25, 73 and 77; *Mikasa*, Secaucus, NJ on pages 23, 65 and 83; *Mottahedeh*, New York, NY on pages 29, 48-49 and 87; *Oneida Silversmiths*, Oneida, NY on page 19.

*Swanson Broths are at least 99% fat free.

NO FAT* ADDED

recipes

▼

Keep meals simple and satisfying without extra fat. Trimming fat from the diet is a snap when you choose recipes like *Chicken Primavera, Zesty Turkey and Rice* and *Easy Pepper Steak.* The secret is using delicious SWANSON Broth to help provide the flavor and moistness that fat usually supplies. Whether it's a main dish, soup, vegetable or salad — here's a mouthwatering collection of recipes to fit menus for family meals or company fare!

*Swanson Broths are at least 99% fat free.

Lemon Herb Chicken, left (page 6) and *Sesame Vegetables and Noodles,* right (page 7).

LEMON HERB CHICKEN

1 can (14½ ounces) SWANSON Chicken Broth
3 tablespoons lemon juice
1 teaspoon dried basil leaves, crushed
1 teaspoon dried thyme leaves, crushed
⅛ teaspoon pepper
4 chicken breast halves (about 2 pounds), skinned

▶ In bowl mix broth, lemon juice, basil, thyme and pepper. Set aside.
▶ Place chicken on lightly oiled grill rack over medium-hot coals. Grill uncovered 20 minutes, turning often. Brush with broth mixture and grill 20 minutes more or until chicken is no longer pink, turning and brushing often with broth mixture.

Serves 4 • Prep Time: 5 minutes • Cook Time: 40 minutes

Nutritional Values Per Serving: Calories 155, Total Fat 4g, Saturated Fat 1g, Cholesterol 73mg, Sodium 506mg, Total Carbohydrate 2g, Protein 27g

Herb Broiled Chicken: Prepare as in first step. Place chicken on rack in broiler pan. Broil 6 inches from heat 30 minutes or until chicken is no longer pink, turning and brushing often with broth mixture.

Basting the chicken with rich-tasting SWANSON Broth, spiked with lemon and seasonings, helps keep the chicken moist and flavorful.

SESAME VEGETABLES AND NOODLES

6 ounces dry linguine
2 cups broccoli flowerets
2 medium carrots, sliced (about 1 cup)
1 medium red *or* green pepper, diced (about 1 cup)
2 tablespoons cornstarch
1 can (14½ ounces) SWANSON Oriental Broth
1 tablespoon Louisiana-style hot sauce
¼ teaspoon garlic powder *or* 2 cloves garlic, minced
2 green onions, sliced (about ¼ cup)
1 tablespoon toasted sesame seed

▶ In large saucepan prepare linguine according to package directions without salt. Add broccoli, carrots and pepper for last 5 minutes of cooking time. Drain in colander.
▶ In same pan mix cornstarch, broth, hot sauce and garlic powder until smooth. Over medium heat, cook until mixture boils and thickens, stirring constantly. Add linguine mixture, onions and sesame seed. Heat through, stirring occasionally.

Serves 4 • Prep Time: 15 minutes • Cook Time: 20 minutes

Nutritional Values Per Serving: Calories 229, Total Fat 2g, Saturated Fat 0g, Cholesterol 1mg, Sodium 524mg, Total Carbohydrate 45g, Protein 8g

STEAMED VEGETABLES

1 can (14½ ounces) SWANSON Vegetable Broth
3 cups cut-up vegetables*

▶ In medium saucepan over medium-high heat, heat broth and vegetables to a boil. Reduce heat to low. Cover and cook 5 minutes or until vegetables are tender. Drain.

Serves 4 • Prep Time: 10 minutes • Cook Time: 10 minutes

*Use a combination of broccoli flowerets, cauliflower flowerets, sliced carrot and sliced celery.

Nutritional Values Per Serving: Calories 38, Total Fat 1g, Saturated Fat 0g, Cholesterol 0mg, Sodium 523mg, Total Carbohydrate 7g, Protein 2g

GLAZED CHICKEN AND ORIENTAL VEGETABLES

2 tablespoons cornstarch
1 can (14½ ounces) SWANSON Oriental Broth
1 tablespoon honey
1 teaspoon dry mustard
4 skinless, boneless chicken breast halves (about 1 pound)
1 large carrot, cut into 2-inch matchstick-thin strips (about 1 cup)
1 package (4 ounces) snow peas (about 1 cup)
4 cups hot cooked rice, cooked without salt

▶ In bowl mix cornstarch, broth, honey and mustard until smooth. Set aside.
▶ In medium nonstick skillet over medium-high heat, cook chicken 10 minutes or until browned. Set chicken aside.
▶ Stir cornstarch mixture and add. Cook until mixture boils and thickens, stirring constantly. Return chicken to pan. Add carrot and snow peas. Reduce heat to low. Cover and cook 5 minutes or until chicken is no longer pink. Serve with rice. If desired, garnish with *cracked pepper.*

Serves 4 • Prep Time: 10 minutes • Cook Time: 20 minutes

Nutritional Values Per Serving: Calories 449, Total Fat 4g, Saturated Fat 1g, Cholesterol 73mg, Sodium 568mg, Total Carbohydrate 67g, Protein 33g

S*WANSON Oriental Broth*

provides the sauce with an authentic background

flavor that enhances the entire

dish without added fat.

▲ Glazed Chicken and Oriental Vegetables

CHICKEN PRIMAVERA

2 tablespoons cornstarch
1 can (14½ ounces) SWANSON Chicken Broth
¼ teaspoon garlic powder *or* 2 cloves garlic, minced
2 cups broccoli flowerets
2 medium carrots, sliced (about 1 cup)
½ cup green *and/or* red pepper cut in 2-inch-long strips
1 small onion, chopped (about ¼ cup)
2 cups cubed cooked chicken
4 cups hot cooked spaghetti (about 8 ounces dry), cooked without salt
¼ cup shredded Parmesan cheese

▶ In cup mix cornstarch and *¼ cup* broth until smooth. Set aside.
▶ In medium saucepan mix remaining broth, garlic powder, broccoli, carrots, pepper and onion. Over medium-high heat, heat to a boil. Reduce heat to low. Cover and cook 5 minutes or until vegetables are tender-crisp.
▶ Stir cornstarch mixture and add. Cook until mixture boils and thickens, stirring constantly. Add chicken and heat through. Toss with spaghetti and cheese.

Serves 4 • Prep Time: 15 minutes • Cook Time: 20 minutes

Nutritional Values Per Serving: Calories 400, Total Fat 8g, Saturated Fat 3g, Cholesterol 57mg, Sodium 613mg, Total Carbohydrate 52g, Protein 29g

Pasta's principal nutrient is complex carbohydrate, and it's naturally low in fat. Tender-crisp vegetables in a light, smooth sauce meld the pasta and chicken into one delicious dish!

▲ Chicken Primavera

ONE-DISH CHICKEN AND RICE

1 pound skinless, boneless chicken breasts, cut into cubes
1 can (14½ ounces) SWANSON Chicken Broth
½ teaspoon dried basil leaves, crushed
½ teaspoon garlic powder
¾ cup uncooked regular long-grain rice
1 bag (16 ounces) frozen vegetable combination

▶ In medium nonstick skillet over medium-high heat, cook chicken in 2 batches until browned, stirring often. Set chicken aside.
▶ Stir in broth, basil and garlic powder. Heat to a boil. Stir in rice. Reduce heat to low. Cover and cook 5 minutes.
▶ Return chicken to pan. Stir in vegetables. Cover and cook 15 minutes more or until rice is done and most of liquid is absorbed. If desired, garnish with *lemon peel* and *paprika*.

Serves 4 • Prep Time: 10 minutes • Cook Time: 35 minutes

Nutritional Values Per Serving: Calories 300, Total Fat 4g, Saturated Fat 1g, Cholesterol 73mg, Sodium 535mg, Total Carbohydrate 29g, Protein 31g

CHICKEN BROCCOLI DIJON

4 skinless, boneless chicken breast halves (about 1 pound)
1 can (14½ ounces) SWANSON Chicken Broth
⅛ teaspoon garlic powder *or* 1 clove garlic, minced
2 cups broccoli flowerets
¼ cup all-purpose flour
½ cup milk
1 tablespoon Dijon-style mustard
4 cups hot cooked medium egg noodles (about 4 cups dry), cooked without salt

▶ In medium nonstick skillet over medium-high heat, cook chicken 10 minutes or until browned. Set chicken aside.
▶ Add broth, garlic powder and broccoli. Heat to a boil. Return chicken to pan. Reduce heat to low. Cover and cook 5 minutes or until chicken is no longer pink. Set chicken aside and keep warm.
▶ In cup mix flour, milk and mustard until smooth. Gradually add to broth mixture. Cook until mixture boils and thickens, stirring constantly. Serve with chicken and noodles.

Serves 4 • Prep Time: 10 minutes • Cook Time: 25 minutes

Nutritional Values Per Serving: Calories 426, Total Fat 7g, Saturated Fat 2g, Cholesterol 128mg, Sodium 631mg, Total Carbohydrate 50g, Protein 38g

▲ One-Dish Chicken and Rice

CHICKEN KABOBS

3 tablespoons cornstarch
1 can (14½ ounces) SWANSON Oriental Broth
3 tablespoons sugar
2 tablespoons vinegar
1 pound skinless, boneless chicken breasts, cut into 1-inch pieces
1 medium red *or* green pepper, cut into 1-inch pieces (about 1 cup)
1 can (about 8 ounces) pineapple chunks in juice, drained*
4 cups hot cooked rice, cooked without salt

▶ In small saucepan mix cornstarch, broth, sugar and vinegar until smooth. Over medium heat, cook until mixture boils and thickens, stirring constantly.

▶ On 4 long skewers, thread chicken, pepper and pineapple alternately.

▶ Place kabobs on lightly oiled grill rack over medium-hot coals. Grill uncovered 15 minutes or until chicken is no longer pink, turning and brushing often with broth mixture.

▶ Heat remaining broth mixture to a boil. Serve with kabobs and rice. If desired, garnish rice with *fresh parsley* and *fresh rosemary.*

Serves 4 • Prep Time: 15 minutes • Cook Time: 20 minutes

Nutritional Values Per Serving: Calories 494, Total Fat 4g, Saturated Fat 1g, Cholesterol 73mg, Sodium 563mg, Total Carbohydrate 76g, Protein 32g

Broiled Chicken Kabobs: Prepare as in first and second steps. In third step, place kabobs on rack in broiler pan. Broil 4 inches from heat 15 minutes or until chicken is no longer pink, turning and brushing often with broth mixture. Proceed as in fourth step.

* You may substitute 1½ cups fresh pineapple chunks for canned pineapple.

▲ Chicken Kabobs

QUICK CHICKEN AND NOODLES

  4 skinless, boneless chicken breast halves (about 1 pound)
  ¼ teaspoon garlic powder
  ⅛ teaspoon paprika
  1 can (14½ ounces) SWANSON Chicken Broth
  ½ teaspoon dried basil leaves, crushed
  ⅛ teaspoon pepper
  2 cups frozen vegetable combination (broccoli, cauliflower, carrots)
  2 cups dry wide egg noodles

▶ In medium nonstick skillet over medium-high heat, cook chicken 10 minutes or until browned. Sprinkle with garlic powder and paprika. Set chicken aside.

▶ Add broth, basil, pepper and vegetables. Heat to a boil. Stir in noodles. Return chicken to pan. Reduce heat to low. Cover and cook 10 minutes or until chicken is no longer pink. If desired, garnish with *fresh basil*.

Serves 4 • Prep Time: 5 minutes • Cook Time: 25 minutes

Nutritional Values Per Serving: Calories 245, Total Fat 4g, Saturated Fat 1g, Cholesterol 91mg, Sodium 528mg, Total Carbohydrate 18g, Protein 32g

HERBED BROWN RICE AND CHICKEN

  4 skinless, boneless chicken breast halves (about 1 pound)
  ¼ teaspoon garlic powder
  ⅛ teaspoon pepper
  1 can (14½ ounces) SWANSON NATURAL GOODNESS Chicken Broth
  ½ teaspoon dried thyme leaves, crushed
1½ cups uncooked quick-cooking brown rice
  1 cup frozen peas
  ¼ cup grated Parmesan cheese

▶ In medium nonstick skillet over medium-high heat, cook chicken 10 minutes or until browned. Sprinkle with garlic powder and pepper. Set chicken aside.

▶ Stir in broth and thyme. Heat to a boil. Stir in rice. Reduce heat to low. Cover and cook 5 minutes. Return chicken to pan. Add peas. Cover and cook 5 minutes more or until chicken is no longer pink and rice is done. Remove chicken. Stir cheese into rice mixture.

Serves 4 • Prep Time: 5 minutes • Cook Time: 25 minutes

Nutritional Values Per Serving: Calories 317, Total Fat 6g, Saturated Fat 2g, Cholesterol 77mg, Sodium 489mg, Total Carbohydrate 30g, Protein 35g

▲ Quick Chicken and Noodles

ORANGE-GLAZED CHICKEN

3 tablespoons cornstarch
1 can (14½ ounces) SWANSON Vegetable Broth
1 teaspoon lemon juice
½ cup sweet orange marmalade *or* apple jelly
6 skinless, boneless chicken breast halves (about 1½ pounds)
6 cups hot cooked rice, cooked without salt

▶ In bowl mix cornstarch, broth, lemon juice and marmalade until smooth. Set aside.

▶ In medium nonstick skillet over medium-high heat, cook chicken in 2 batches 10 minutes or until browned. Set chicken aside.

▶ Stir cornstarch mixture and add. Cook until mixture boils and thickens, stirring constantly. Return chicken to pan. Reduce heat to low. Cover and cook 5 minutes or until chicken is no longer pink. Serve with rice. If desired, garnish rice with *fresh parsley* and chicken with *fresh thyme*.

Serves 6 • Prep Time: 5 minutes • Cook Time: 30 minutes

Nutritional Values Per Serving: Calories 435, Total Fat 4g, Saturated Fat 1g, Cholesterol 73mg, Sodium 387mg, Total Carbohydrate 65g, Protein 32g

You'll never miss the fat in this tasty chicken entrée with a touch of sweetness and the full flavor of SWANSON Broth.

▲ Orange-Glazed Chicken

CHICKEN BROCCOLI TWIST

3 cups dry corkscrew macaroni
2 cups broccoli flowerets
2 medium carrots, sliced (about 1 cup)
1 can (10¾ ounces) CAMPBELL'S HEALTHY REQUEST condensed
  Cream of Broccoli Soup
1 can (14½ ounces) SWANSON NATURAL GOODNESS Chicken Broth
½ teaspoon garlic powder
⅛ teaspoon pepper
2 cups cubed cooked chicken
¼ cup shredded Parmesan cheese

▶ In large saucepan prepare macaroni according to package directions, omitting salt. Add broccoli and carrots for last 5 minutes of cooking time. Drain in colander.

▶ In same pan mix soup, broth, garlic powder, pepper, chicken and macaroni mixture. Over medium heat, heat through, stirring occasionally. Sprinkle with cheese. If desired, garnish with *fresh thyme*.

Serves 5 • Prep Time: 10 minutes • Cook Time: 20 minutes

Nutritional Values Per Serving: Calories 408, Total Fat 7g, Saturated Fat 2g, Cholesterol 47mg, Sodium 577mg, Total Carbohydrate 57g, Protein 27g

L*ow fat doesn't have to mean no fat.*

There's room for some fat even on a low-fat diet.

In fact, nutrients called essential fatty acids come

from fat and are needed in small quantities

as part of a healthy diet.

▲ Chicken Broccoli Twist

MARINATED TURKEY BREAST

4½ to 5-pound turkey breast
1 can (14½ ounces) SWANSON NATURAL GOODNESS Chicken Broth
1 teaspoon dried rosemary leaves, crushed
1 teaspoon dried thyme leaves, crushed
⅛ teaspoon pepper

▶ Rinse turkey with cold water and pat dry. Mix broth, rosemary, thyme and pepper in large deep nonmetallic dish. Add turkey and turn to coat. Cover and refrigerate 2 hours, turning turkey occasionally.

▶ Remove turkey from marinade and place meat-side up on rack in shallow roasting pan. Insert meat thermometer into thickest part of meat, not touching bone.

▶ Roast at 350°F. for 1¾ to 2½ hours or until thermometer reads 170°F., basting occasionally with marinade. Begin checking doneness after 1½ hours roasting time. Allow turkey to stand 10 minutes before slicing.

Serves 6 to 8 • Prep Time: 10 minutes • Marinating Time: 2 hours
Cook Time: 1¾ to 2½ hours • Stand Time: 10 minutes

Nutritional Values Per Serving: Calories 122, Total Fat 1g, Saturated Fat 0g, Cholesterol 71mg, Sodium 233mg, Total Carbohydrate 1g, Protein 26g

If a marinade is to be used as a sauce or gravy, it must be brought to a rolling boil and cooked for several minutes before serving.

▲ Marinated Turkey Breast

ZESTY TURKEY AND RICE

1 **can (14½ ounces) SWANSON NATURAL GOODNESS Chicken Broth**
1 **teaspoon dried basil leaves, crushed**
¼ **teaspoon garlic powder**
¼ **teaspoon hot pepper sauce**
1 **can (about 14½ ounces) stewed tomatoes**
¾ **cup uncooked regular long-grain rice**
1 **cup frozen peas**
2 **cups cubed cooked turkey** *or* **chicken**

▶ In medium saucepan mix broth, basil, garlic powder, hot pepper sauce and tomatoes. Over medium-high heat, heat to a boil. Stir in rice. Reduce heat to low. Cover and cook 20 minutes.

▶ Stir in peas and turkey. Cover and cook 5 minutes or until rice is done.

Serves 4 • Prep Time: 5 minutes • Cook Time: 30 minutes

Nutritional Values Per Serving: Calories 290, Total Fat 3g, Saturated Fat 1g, Cholesterol 69mg, Sodium 535mg, Total Carbohydrate 38g, Protein 27g

CHICKEN MUSHROOM RISOTTO

¾ **pound skinless, boneless chicken breasts, cut into cubes**
1 **small onion, finely chopped (about ¼ cup)**
1 **small carrot, chopped (about ¼ cup)**
1 **cup uncooked regular long-grain rice**
1 **can (10¾ ounces) CAMPBELL'S HEALTHY REQUEST condensed Cream of Mushroom Soup**
1 **can (14½ ounces) SWANSON NATURAL GOODNESS Chicken Broth**
⅛ **teaspoon pepper**
½ **cup frozen peas**

▶ In medium nonstick skillet over medium-high heat, cook chicken until browned, stirring often. Set chicken aside.

▶ Reduce heat to medium. Add onion and carrot. Add rice and cook until rice is browned, stirring constantly.

▶ Stir in soup, broth and pepper. Heat to a boil. Reduce heat to low. Cover and cook 15 minutes, stirring occasionally.

▶ Return chicken to pan. Add peas. Cover and cook 5 minutes more or until chicken and rice are done and most of liquid is absorbed.

Serves 4 • Prep Time: 10 minutes • Cook Time: 35 minutes

Nutritional Values Per Serving: Calories 359, Total Fat 4g, Saturated Fat 1g, Cholesterol 55mg, Sodium 661mg, Total Carbohydrate 52g, Protein 26g

▲ Zesty Turkey and Rice

BEEF AND PASTA

¾ pound lean ground beef (85% lean)
1 can (14½ ounces) SWANSON Vegetable Broth
1 tablespoon Worcestershire sauce
½ teaspoon dried oregano leaves, crushed
½ teaspoon garlic powder
1 can (about 8 ounces) stewed tomatoes
1½ cups dry medium tube-shaped *or* corkscrew macaroni

▶ In medium skillet over medium-high heat, cook beef until browned, stirring to separate meat. Pour off fat.

▶ Add broth, Worcestershire, oregano, garlic powder and tomatoes. Heat to a boil. Stir in macaroni. Reduce heat to low. Cover and cook 10 minutes, stirring often.

▶ Uncover and cook 5 minutes more or until macaroni is done and most of liquid is absorbed. If desired, garnish with *Parmesan cheese.*

Serves 4 • Prep Time: 5 minutes • Cook Time: 25 minutes

Nutritional Values Per Serving: Calories 307, Total Fat 11g, Saturated Fat 4g, Cholesterol 59mg, Sodium 692mg, Total Carbohydrate 29g, Protein 21g

B*y controlling portion size*

(2 to 3 ounces cooked is recommended),

lean cuts of beef like round steak, short loin

and well-drained lean ground beef can be

made to fit into a low-fat diet.

▲ Beef and Pasta

SHORTCUT SWISS STEAK

1 pound boneless beef top round steak, ¾ inch thick
3 tablespoons cornstarch
1 can (14½ ounces) SWANSON Beef Broth
½ teaspoon garlic powder
½ teaspoon sugar
1 cup cut-up canned tomatoes
1 medium onion, cut into wedges
1 stalk celery, sliced (about ½ cup)
4 cups hot cooked wide egg noodles (about 4 cups dry),
    cooked without salt

▶ Slice beef into very thin strips. In bowl mix cornstarch and *1 cup* broth until smooth. Set aside.

▶ In medium nonstick skillet over medium-high heat, cook beef in 2 batches until browned, stirring often. Set beef aside.

▶ Add remaining broth, garlic powder, sugar, tomatoes, onion and celery. Heat to a boil. Reduce heat to low. Cover and cook 5 minutes or until vegetables are tender-crisp.

▶ Stir cornstarch mixture and add. Cook until mixture boils and thickens, stirring constantly. Return beef to pan and heat through. Serve over noodles.

Serves 4 • Prep Time: 15 minutes • Cook Time: 25 minutes

Nutritional Values Per Serving: Calories 443, Total Fat 8g, Saturated Fat 2g, Cholesterol 127mg, Sodium 618mg, Total Carbohydrate 53g, Protein 38g

Choose a variety of foods to create a well-balanced diet, remembering to keep fat intake and calories in check.

▲ Shortcut Swiss Steak

EASY PEPPER STEAK

1 pound boneless beef top round steak, ¾ inch thick
3 tablespoons cornstarch
1 can (14½ ounces) SWANSON Beef Broth
1 tablespoon soy sauce
¼ teaspoon garlic powder *or* 2 cloves garlic, minced
2 small green *and/or* red peppers, cut into 2-inch-long strips (about 2 cups)
1 medium onion, cut into wedges
4 cups hot cooked rice, cooked without salt

▶ Slice beef into very thin strips. In bowl mix cornstarch and *1 cup* broth until smooth. Set aside.

▶ In medium nonstick skillet over medium-high heat, cook beef in 2 batches until browned, stirring often. Set beef aside.

▶ Add remaining broth, soy, garlic powder, peppers and onion. Heat to a boil. Reduce heat to low. Cover and cook 5 minutes or until vegetables are tender-crisp.

▶ Stir cornstarch mixture and add. Cook until mixture boils and thickens, stirring constantly. Return beef to pan and heat through. Serve over rice. If desired, garnish with *fresh thyme.*

Serves 4 • Prep Time: 15 minutes • Cook Time: 25 minutes

Nutritional Values Per Serving: Calories 466, Total Fat 6g, Saturated Fat 2g, Cholesterol 74mg, Sodium 755mg, Total Carbohydrate 64g, Protein 35g

Well-trimmed lean cuts of beef, like top round steak and tenderloin, are good choices for stir-frys.

▲ Easy Pepper Steak

BEAN AND RICE BURRITOS

Vegetable cooking spray
1 medium onion, chopped (about ½ cup)
1 can (16 ounces) CAMPBELL'S Pork & Beans in Tomato Sauce
⅓ cup PACE Thick & Chunky Salsa
¼ cup shredded Cheddar cheese (1 ounce)
1½ cups cooked rice, cooked without salt
6 flour tortillas (8-inch)

▶ Spray medium saucepan with cooking spray and heat over medium heat 1 minute. Add onion and cook until tender.
▶ Add beans, salsa, cheese and rice. Heat through, stirring occasionally.
▶ Warm tortillas according to package directions. Spoon ½ cup bean mixture down center of each tortilla. Fold tortilla around filling.

Makes 6 burritos • Prep Time: 20 minutes • Cook Time: 10 minutes

Nutritional Values Per Serving: Calories 282, Total Fat 5g, Saturated Fat 2g, Cholesterol 5mg, Sodium 610mg, Total Carbohydrate 49g, Protein 9g

MUSTARD PORK CHOPS

3 tablespoons cornstarch
1 can (14½ ounces) SWANSON Beef Broth
1 tablespoon spicy-brown mustard
Vegetable cooking spray
6 boneless pork chops, ¾ inch thick (about 1½ pounds)
2 cups sliced mushrooms (about 6 ounces)
1 medium onion, sliced (about ½ cup)
6 cups hot cooked rice, cooked without salt

▶ In bowl mix cornstarch, broth and mustard until smooth. Set aside.
▶ Spray medium skillet with cooking spray and heat over medium-high heat 1 minute. Add chops in 2 batches and cook 10 minutes or until browned. Set chops aside.
▶ Remove pan from heat. Spray with cooking spray. Reduce heat to medium. Add mushrooms and onion and cook until tender and liquid is evaporated, stirring often.
▶ Stir cornstarch mixture and add. Cook until mixture boils and thickens, stirring constantly. Return chops to pan. Reduce heat to low. Cover and cook 5 minutes or until chops are no longer pink. Serve with rice.

Serves 6 • Prep Time: 15 minutes • Cook Time: 35 minutes

Nutritional Values Per Serving: Calories 447, Total Fat 8g, Saturated Fat 3g, Cholesterol 68mg, Sodium 369mg, Total Carbohydrate 59g, Protein 30g

▲ Bean and Rice Burritos

POACHED FISH FILLETS

4   teaspoons cornstarch
1   can (14½ ounces) SWANSON Vegetable Broth
¼   teaspoon dried dill weed, crushed
    Generous dash pepper
1   large carrot, cut into 2-inch matchstick-thin strips (about 1 cup)
1   stalk celery, sliced (about ½ cup)
1   small yellow *or* red onion, cut into wedges
1   pound fresh *or* thawed frozen firm white-fish fillets*

▶ In cup mix cornstarch and *¼ cup* broth until smooth. Set aside.
▶ In medium skillet mix remaining broth, dill weed, pepper, carrot, celery and onion. Over medium-high heat, heat to a boil. Reduce heat to low. Cover and cook 5 minutes or until vegetables are tender-crisp.
▶ Place fish in broth mixture. Cover and cook 5 minutes or until fish flakes easily when tested with a fork. Remove fish and keep warm.
▶ Stir cornstarch mixture and add. Cook until mixture boils and thickens, stirring constantly. Serve with fish. If desired, garnish with *fresh dill* and *green onion.*

Serves 4 • Prep Time: 15 minutes • Cook Time: 20 minutes

Nutritional Values Per Serving: Calories 150, Total Fat 6g, Saturated Fat 1g, Cholesterol 55mg, Sodium 505mg, Total Carbohydrate 6g, Protein 18g

* Use cod, haddock *or* halibut.

QUICK VEGETABLE RICE SOUP

2   cans (14½ ounces *each*) SWANSON NATURAL GOODNESS Chicken Broth
1   medium carrot, sliced (about ½ cup)
1   stalk celery, coarsely chopped (about ½ cup)
¼   cup uncooked regular long-grain rice

In medium saucepan mix broth, carrot and celery. Over medium-high heat, heat to a boil. Stir in rice. Reduce heat to low. Cover and cook 20 minutes or until rice is done, stirring occasionally.

Serves 4 • Prep Time: 10 minutes • Cook Time: 25 minutes

Nutritional Values Per Serving: Calories 72, Total Fat 1g, Saturated Fat 0g, Cholesterol 0mg, Sodium 578mg, Total Carbohydrate 13g, Protein 3g

▲ Poached Fish Fillets

QUICK CHILI AND RICE

1½ pounds lean ground beef (85% lean)
1 large onion, chopped (about 1 cup)
2 tablespoons chili powder
¼ teaspoon ground red pepper
3 cups V8 100% Vegetable Juice
2 cans (16 ounces *each*) CAMPBELL'S Pork & Beans in Tomato Sauce
8 cups hot cooked rice, cooked without salt

▶ In Dutch oven over medium-high heat, cook beef, onion, chili powder and pepper until beef is browned, stirring to separate meat. Pour off fat.
▶ Add vegetable juice and beans. Heat to a boil. Reduce heat to low. Cook 10 minutes, stirring occasionally. Serve over rice. If desired, garnish with *green onion.*

Serves 8 • Prep Time: 10 minutes • Cook Time: 25 minutes

Nutritional Values Per Serving: Calories 555, Total Fat 13g, Saturated Fat 5g, Cholesterol 59mg, Sodium 671mg, Total Carbohydrate 80g, Protein 28g

R*eady to eat in 35 minutes, yet it tastes like it simmered all day. Vitamin A in this dish comes from the "V8" juice, the tomato sauce and (perhaps surprisingly) the chili powder.*

▲ Quick Chili and Rice

CHICKEN VEGETABLE SOUP

3 cans (14½ ounces *each*) SWANSON NATURAL GOODNESS
   Chicken Broth
½ teaspoon dried thyme leaves, crushed
¼ teaspoon garlic powder *or* 2 cloves garlic, minced
2 cups frozen whole kernel corn
1 package (about 10 ounces) frozen cut green beans (about 2 cups)
1 cup cut-up canned tomatoes
1 stalk celery, chopped (about ½ cup)
2 cups cubed cooked chicken

▶ In large saucepan mix broth, thyme, garlic powder, corn, beans, tomatoes and celery. Over medium-high heat, heat to a boil. Reduce heat to low. Cover and cook 5 minutes or until vegetables are tender.

▶ Add chicken and heat through.

Serves 6 • Prep Time: 10 minutes • Cook Time: 20 minutes

Nutritional Values Per Serving: Calories 174, Total Fat 4g, Saturated Fat 1g, Cholesterol 35mg, Sodium 664mg, Total Carbohydrate 20g, Protein 17g

Soups are the perfect opportunity to add a variety of vegetables — and the vitamins, minerals and fiber they provide — without adding fat.

▲ Chicken Vegetable Soup

HERBED SKILLET VEGETABLES

  2 tablespoons cornstarch
  1 can (14½ ounces) SWANSON NATURAL GOODNESS Chicken Broth
  ½ teaspoon dried thyme leaves, crushed
  ⅛ teaspoon pepper
 12 small new potatoes (about 1¼ pounds), cut into quarters
  2 medium carrots, cut into 1-inch pieces (about 1 cup)
  2 stalks celery, cut into 2-inch pieces (about 1½ cups)

▶ In cup mix cornstarch and ¼ *cup* broth until smooth. Set aside.

▶ In medium skillet mix remaining broth, thyme, pepper, potatoes, carrots and celery. Over medium-high heat, heat to a boil. Reduce heat to low. Cover and cook 20 minutes or until vegetables are tender. With slotted spoon, remove vegetables to serving dish.

▶ Stir reserved cornstarch mixture and add. Cook until mixture boils and thickens, stirring constantly. Serve over vegetables.

Serves 4 • Prep Time: 15 minutes • Cook Time: 30 minutes

Nutritional Values Per Serving: Calories 213, Total Fat 1g, Saturated Fat 0g, Cholesterol 0mg, Sodium 330mg, Total Carbohydrate 48g, Protein 5g

LENTIL RICE SALAD

  1 can (14½ ounces) SWANSON Chicken Broth
  ½ cup uncooked regular long-grain rice
  ⅓ cup dried lentils
  2 tablespoons chopped fresh parsley
     Generous dash ground red pepper
  1 stalk celery, sliced (about ½ cup)
  1 medium red onion, chopped (about ½ cup)
  ½ cup diced green *or* red pepper
  ½ cup refrigerated MARIE'S Zesty Fat Free Italian Vinaigrette
     Lettuce leaves

▶ In medium saucepan over medium-high heat, heat broth to a boil. Stir in rice and lentils. Reduce heat to low. Cover and cook 20 minutes or until rice is done. Let stand 5 minutes or until liquid is absorbed.

▶ In large bowl toss lentil mixture, parsley, ground red pepper, celery, onion, green pepper and vinaigrette until evenly coated. Refrigerate at least 2 hours or overnight. Serve on lettuce.

Serves 6 • Prep Time: 35 minutes • Chill Time: 2 hours

Nutritional Values Per Serving: Calories 131, Total Fat 1g, Saturated Fat 0g, Cholesterol 0mg, Sodium 449mg, Total Carbohydrate 26g, Protein 5g

▲ Herbed Skillet Vegetables

SPAGHETTI FLORENTINE

  1   can (14½ ounces) SWANSON Chicken Broth
  ⅓   cup all-purpose flour
  ½   teaspoon Italian seasoning, crushed
  ¼   teaspoon garlic powder *or* 2 cloves garlic, minced
  ⅛   teaspoon pepper
  1   package (about 10 ounces) frozen chopped spinach, thawed
       and *well* drained
  ½   cup plain yogurt
  1   medium tomato, diced (about 1 cup)
  4   cups hot cooked spaghetti (about 8 ounces dry), cooked without salt
  ¼   cup grated Parmesan cheese

▶ In medium saucepan gradually mix broth into flour, Italian seasoning, garlic powder and pepper until smooth. Add spinach. Over medium heat, cook until mixture boils and thickens, stirring constantly.

▶ Remove from heat. Stir in yogurt and tomato. Toss with spaghetti. Sprinkle with cheese. If desired, garnish with *fresh parsley*.

Serves 6 • Prep Time: 20 minutes • Cook Time: 5 minutes

Nutritional Values Per Serving: Calories 210, Total Fat 3g, Saturated Fat 1g, Cholesterol 4mg, Sodium 420mg, Total Carbohydrate 37g, Protein 10g

APPLE RAISIN STUFFING

  1   can (14½ ounces) SWANSON NATURAL GOODNESS Chicken Broth
  ¼   cup apple juice
  ½   cup raisins
  1   stalk celery, sliced (about ½ cup)
  1   medium onion, chopped (about ½ cup)
  5   cups PEPPERIDGE FARM Cubed Herb Seasoned Stuffing

▶ In large saucepan mix broth, apple juice, raisins, celery and onion. Over medium-high heat, heat to a boil. Reduce heat to low. Cover and cook 5 minutes or until vegetables are tender. Remove from heat. Add stuffing. Mix lightly.

▶ Spoon into 1½-quart casserole. Bake at 350°F. for 20 minutes or until hot.

Serves 8 • Prep Time: 15 minutes • Cook Time: 20 minutes

Nutritional Values Per Serving: Calories 157, Total Fat 1g, Saturated Fat 0g, Cholesterol 0mg, Sodium 588mg, Total Carbohydrate 33g, Protein 4g

▲ Spaghetti Florentine

SOUTHWESTERN BEAN AND RICE MEDLEY

Vegetable cooking spray
1 medium onion, chopped (about ½ cup)
1 small green pepper, chopped (about ½ cup)
2 teaspoons chili powder
2 cans (16 ounces *each*) CAMPBELL'S Pork & Beans in Tomato Sauce
⅛ teaspoon hot pepper sauce (optional)
1 cup frozen whole kernel corn
1½ cups cooked rice, cooked without salt

▶ Spray medium saucepan with cooking spray and heat over medium heat 1 minute. Add onion, pepper and chili powder and cook until tender-crisp.
▶ Add beans, hot pepper sauce, corn and rice. Heat to a boil. Reduce heat to low. Cook 5 minutes or until corn is tender, stirring occasionally. If desired, garnish with *red pepper*, *green onion* and *ripe olives*.

Serves 6 • Prep Time: 10 minutes • Cook Time: 15 minutes

Nutritional Values Per Serving: Calories 251, Total Fat 2g, Saturated Fat 1g, Cholesterol 1mg, Sodium 501mg, Total Carbohydrate 49g, Protein 9g

VEGETABLE RICE AND BEANS

1 can (14½ ounces) SWANSON Vegetable Broth
1 tablespoon chili powder
¼ teaspoon garlic powder
⅛ teaspoon pepper
3 medium carrots, chopped (about 1 cup)
2 small zucchini, coarsely chopped (about 2 cups)
1 cup uncooked regular long-grain rice
1 can (about 16 ounces) black beans, rinsed and drained
1 medium tomato, chopped (about 1 cup)

▶ In large saucepan mix broth, chili powder, garlic powder, pepper, carrots and zucchini. Over medium-high heat, heat to a boil. Stir in rice. Reduce heat to low. Cover and cook 20 minutes or until rice is done and most of liquid is absorbed.
▶ Add beans and tomato and heat through.

Serves 6 • Prep Time: 10 minutes • Cook Time: 30 minutes

Nutritional Values Per Serving: Calories 204, Total Fat 1g, Saturated Fat 0g, Cholesterol 0mg, Sodium 423mg, Total Carbohydrate 42g, Protein 7g

▲ Southwestern Bean and Rice Medley

MARINATED VEGETABLES

1   can (14½ ounces) SWANSON Vegetable Broth
1   tablespoon sugar
½   teaspoon dried thyme leaves, crushed
¼   teaspoon garlic powder *or* 2 cloves garlic, minced
⅛   teaspoon pepper
4   cups cauliflower flowerets (about 1 small head)
½   pound green beans, cut into 1-inch pieces (about 1½ cups)
2   medium carrots, sliced (about 1 cup)
¼   cup vinegar
2   tablespoons chopped fresh parsley *or* 2 teaspoons dried parsley flakes

▶ In large saucepan over medium-high heat, heat broth, sugar, thyme, garlic powder and pepper to a boil. Add cauliflower, beans and carrots. Reduce heat to low. Cover and cook 1 minute or until vegetables are tender-crisp.

▶ Place vegetables and broth mixture in shallow nonmetallic dish. Add vinegar and parsley. Refrigerate at least 12 hours, stirring occasionally.

▶ Serve vegetables with slotted spoon. If desired, serve over *lettuce* and *tomato*.

Serves 12 • Prep Time: 15 minutes • Cook Time: 10 minutes
Marinating Time: 12 hours

Nutritional Values Per Serving: Calories 30, Total Fat 0g, Saturated Fat 0g, Cholesterol 0mg, Sodium 157mg, Total Carbohydrate 6g, Protein 1g

Broccoli, cauliflower and Brussels sprouts — cruciferous vegetables — are especially good sources of vitamin C and also supply fiber. It's a healthy idea to include these vegetables in your meals several times each week.

▲ Marinated Vegetables

MAKEOVER
favorites

▼

Following current nutrition guidelines doesn't mean having to say good-bye to traditional favorites. These fresh ideas with SWANSON Broth will show you how to remodel your favorite recipes for today's lower-fat cooking. Try the recipe makeovers for *One-Dish Beef Stroganoff and Noodles, Home-Style Beef Stew* or *Guilt-Free Alfredo.* For new and old recipe favorites, use SWANSON Broth...*when all you want to add is flavor.*

Pictured clockwise from right: *Lemon Honey Chicken and Stuffing* (page 50), *"Unfried" Rice* (page 51) and *Garlic Shrimp and Pasta* (page 51).

LEMON HONEY CHICKEN AND STUFFING

1 can (14½ ounces) SWANSON NATURAL GOODNESS Chicken Broth
2 medium carrots, shredded (about 1 cup)
4 cups PEPPERIDGE FARM Herb Seasoned Stuffing
6 chicken breast halves (about 3 pounds), skinned
2 tablespoons honey
2 tablespoons lemon juice
1 tablespoon chopped fresh parsley *or* 1 teaspoon dried parsley flakes
3 lemon slices

▶ In large saucepan mix broth and carrots. Over medium-high heat, heat to a boil. Remove from heat. Add stuffing. Mix lightly.

▶ Spoon into greased 3-quart shallow baking dish. Arrange chicken over stuffing.

▶ Bake at 375°F. for 50 minutes.

▶ Mix honey, lemon juice and parsley. Brush over chicken. If desired, sprinkle with *paprika*. Cut lemon slices in half and place on chicken. Bake 10 minutes more or until chicken is no longer pink. Remove chicken. Stir stuffing.

Serves 6 • Prep Time: 15 minutes • Cook Time: 1 hour

Nutritional Values Per Serving: Calories 328, Total Fat 5g, Saturated Fat 1g, Cholesterol 73mg, Sodium 788mg, Total Carbohydrate 38g, Protein 32g

A simple step that yields big fat-saving dividends

is removing the skin from chicken breasts.

You can cut the amount of fat in half.

GARLIC SHRIMP AND PASTA

2 tablespoons cornstarch
1 can (14½ ounces) SWANSON Chicken Broth
2 cloves garlic, minced
3 tablespoons chopped fresh parsley *or* 1 tablespoon dried parsley flakes
2 tablespoons lemon juice
⅛ teaspoon ground red pepper
1 pound medium shrimp, shelled and deveined
4 cups hot cooked thin spaghetti (about 8 ounces dry), cooked without salt

▶ In medium saucepan mix cornstarch, broth, garlic, parsley, lemon juice and pepper. Over medium-high heat, cook until mixture boils and thickens, stirring constantly.

▶ Add shrimp. Cook 5 minutes or until shrimp turn pink, stirring often. Toss with spaghetti. If desired, garnish with *lime*.

Serves 4 • Prep Time: 15 minutes • Cook Time: 10 minutes

Nutritional Values Per Serving: Calories 348, Total Fat 4g, Saturated Fat 1g, Cholesterol 173mg, Sodium 614mg, Total Carbohydrate 46g, Protein 31g

"UNFRIED" RICE

   Vegetable cooking spray
1 egg, beaten
¾ cup uncooked regular long-grain rice
1 can (14½ ounces) SWANSON Oriental Broth
¼ teaspoon garlic powder
1 medium carrot, sliced (about ½ cup)
2 green onions, thickly sliced (about ½ cup)
½ cup frozen peas

▶ Spray medium nonstick skillet with cooking spray and heat over medium heat 1 minute. Add egg and cook until set, stirring often. Set egg aside.

▶ Remove skillet from heat. Spray with cooking spray. Add rice and cook until browned, stirring constantly.

▶ Stir in broth, garlic powder and carrot. Heat to a boil. Reduce heat to low. Cover and cook 15 minutes. Add onions and peas. Cook 5 minutes more or until rice is done and most of liquid is absorbed. Stir in egg and heat through.

Serves 4 • Prep Time: 10 minutes • Cook Time: 30 minutes

Nutritional Values Per Serving: Calories 192, Total Fat 2g, Saturated Fat 0g, Cholesterol 54mg, Sodium 521mg, Total Carbohydrate 38g, Protein 6g

COOKS ACROSS AMERICA SHARE THEIR RECIPE TIPS FOR COOKING WITH SWANSON BROTH!

Ms. Fran Hackney   Cherry Hill, NJ
"It's easy to make a lower-fat, rich-tasting 'cream' sauce: Substitute Swanson Chicken Broth and skim milk for the whole milk or cream in your recipe."

Ms. Gigi Langhauser   Decatur, IL
"Steam fresh asparagus for 2 to 3 minutes. While the asparagus is steaming, heat about 1/4 cup Swanson Vegetable Broth and a dash of lemon pepper. Finish cooking the asparagus until tender-crisp in the broth mixture."

Mrs. Vicki Merrick   Hereford, AZ
"Use Swanson Chicken or Beef Broth in place of milk or water when making sauces and gravies. Broth adds delicious flavor with fewer calories than milk and more flavor than water."

Ms. Mary Marti   New Wilmington, PA
"Simmer noodles to succulent plumpness in Swanson Beef, Chicken or Vegetable Broth."

Mrs. Jean Black   North Olmsted, OH
"I make a lower-fat cream sauce for baked chicken by combining Swanson Chicken Broth, low-fat yogurt and a dash of white wine. It's delicious!"

Ms. Karen Cotton   Osage City, KS
"Make a pizza crust the low-fat way — substitute Swanson Chicken or Vegetable Broth for oil and water called for in the recipe."

Mrs. Jeanne Coffin   Plattsburgh, NY
"It's fun to experiment! Swanson Broth can be used to replace most or all of the oil or butter a recipe calls for — with delicious results. And, I have found that substituting the water with Swanson Broth will intensify the flavor."

Ms. Stephanie Krajewski   Secaucus, NJ
"Use Swanson Broth to add delicious flavor to several parts of a turkey dinner. I cook the giblets in Swanson Chicken Broth, substitute Swanson Vegetable Broth for the water in the stuffing, and baste the turkey with Swanson Chicken Broth as it roasts."

Mrs. Donna Haskell   Springfield, MA
"Use a small amount of Swanson Broth instead of butter, margarine or cooking oil when browning food in a nonstick skillet."

Mrs. Nancy Gellhaus   Tucker, GA
"I use Swanson Broth as a base for vegetable soups to boost the flavor and reduce the fat."

▲ "Unfried" Rice (recipe page 51)

CITRUS SKILLET CHICKEN AND RICE

4 skinless, boneless chicken breast halves (about 1 pound)
1 can (14½ ounces) SWANSON Chicken Broth
½ cup orange juice
1 medium onion, chopped (about ½ cup)
1 cup uncooked regular long-grain rice
3 tablespoons chopped fresh parsley *or* 1 tablespoon dried parsley flakes

▶ In medium nonstick skillet over medium-high heat, cook chicken 10 minutes or until browned. Set chicken aside.

▶ Stir in broth, orange juice and onion. Heat to a boil. Stir in rice. Reduce heat to low. Cover and cook 10 minutes.

▶ Return chicken to pan. Cover and cook 10 minutes more or until rice is done and most of liquid is absorbed. Remove chicken to platter. Stir parsley into rice mixture. If desired, garnish with *orange* and *lime peel, red onion* and additional *fresh parsley.*

Serves 4 • Prep Time: 10 minutes • Cook Time: 35 minutes

Nutritional Values Per Serving: Calories 342, Total Fat 4g, Saturated Fat 1g, Cholesterol 73mg, Sodium 508mg, Total Carbohydrate 43g, Protein 31g

A feast for the eyes as well as the palate. Orange juice adds zest and nutrients to this hearty dish that's pretty enough for company.

▲ Citrus Skillet Chicken and Rice

LEMONY CHICKEN PASTA TOSS

2 tablespoons cornstarch
1 can (14½ ounces) SWANSON Chicken Broth
2 tablespoons lemon juice
1 tablespoon Dijon-style mustard
2 cloves garlic, minced
1 pound skinless, boneless chicken breasts, cut into strips
3 tablespoons chopped fresh parsley *or* 1 tablespoon dried parsley flakes
4 cups hot cooked thin spaghetti (about 8 ounces dry), cooked without salt

▶In bowl mix cornstarch, broth, lemon juice, mustard and garlic until smooth. Set aside.

▶In medium nonstick skillet over medium-high heat, cook chicken in 2 batches until browned, stirring often. Set chicken aside.

▶Stir cornstarch mixture and add. Cook until mixture boils and thickens, stirring constantly. Return chicken to pan and heat through. Stir in parsley. Toss with spaghetti. If desired, garnish with *lemon* and *fresh basil*.

Serves 4 • Prep Time: 10 minutes • Cook Time: 20 minutes

Nutritional Values Per Serving: Calories 381, Total Fat 8g, Saturated Fat 2g, Cholesterol 64mg, Sodium 598mg, Total Carbohydrate 46g, Protein 29g

High in complex carbohydrates

and low in fat, pasta is a favorite of athletes.

Besides energy, "enriched" spaghetti and macaroni

provide B vitamins and iron.

▲ Lemony Chicken Pasta Toss

HONEY MUSTARD CHICKEN

2 tablespoons cornstarch

1 can (14½ ounces) SWANSON Chicken Broth

1 tablespoon honey

1 tablespoon Dijon-style *or* coarse-grain mustard

4 skinless, boneless chicken breast halves (about 1 pound)

1 large carrot, cut into 2-inch matchstick-thin strips (about 1 cup)

1 medium yellow *or* red onion, cut into wedges

4 cups hot cooked rice, cooked without salt

▶ In bowl mix cornstarch, broth, honey and mustard until smooth. Set aside.

▶ In medium nonstick skillet over medium-high heat, cook chicken 10 minutes or until browned. Set chicken aside.

▶ Stir cornstarch mixture and add. Cook until mixture boils and thickens, stirring constantly. Return chicken to pan. Add carrot and onion. Reduce heat to low. Cover and cook 5 minutes or until chicken is no longer pink. Serve with rice. If desired, garnish with *green onion.*

Serves 4 • Prep Time: 10 minutes • Cook Time: 20 minutes

Nutritional Values Per Serving: Calories 448, Total Fat 4g, Saturated Fat 1g, Cholesterol 73mg, Sodium 606mg, Total Carbohydrate 65g, Protein 33g

Cut the fat and substitute SWANSON Broth

for the cream and brandy in some mustard sauces.

Tender-crisp matchsticks of carrot add

texture, flavor and vitamin A.

▲ Honey Mustard Chicken

SWEET AND SOUR CHICKEN

3 tablespoons cornstarch
1 can (14½ ounces) SWANSON Oriental Broth
¼ cup vinegar
¼ cup sugar
1 pound skinless, boneless chicken breasts, cut into cubes
1 small green *and/or* red pepper, cut into 2-inch-long strips (about 1 cup)
1 medium carrot, sliced (about ½ cup)
1 can (about 8 ounces) pineapple chunks in juice, drained
4 cups hot cooked rice, cooked without salt

▶ In bowl mix cornstarch, broth, vinegar and sugar until smooth. Set aside.
▶ In medium nonstick skillet over medium-high heat, stir-fry chicken in 2 batches until browned. Set chicken aside.
▶ Stir cornstarch mixture and add. Cook until mixture boils and thickens, stirring constantly. Return chicken to pan. Add pepper, carrot and pineapple. Reduce heat to low. Cover and cook 5 minutes or until chicken is no longer pink. Serve over rice. If desired, garnish with *fresh chives*.

Serves 4 • Prep Time: 15 minutes • Cook Time: 20 minutes

Nutritional Values Per Serving: Calories 498, Total Fat 4g, Saturated Fat 1g, Cholesterol 73mg, Sodium 569mg, Total Carbohydrate 81g, Protein 33g

Sweet and Sour Pork: Substitute 1 pound boneless pork loin, cut into cubes, for the chicken.

Simplify the method and save on fat at the same time! Brown the chicken in a nonstick skillet without added fat. With the rich flavor of SWANSON Oriental Broth, you won't even miss the fat!

▲ Sweet and Sour Chicken

SMOTHERED PORK CHOPS

2 tablespoons cornstarch
1 can (14½ ounces) SWANSON Beef Broth
⅛ teaspoon pepper
  Vegetable cooking spray
6 pork chops, ½ inch thick (about 1½ pounds)
1 medium onion, sliced (about ½ cup)
6 cups hot cooked medium egg noodles (about 6 cups dry),
    cooked without salt

▶ In bowl mix cornstarch, broth and pepper until smooth. Set aside.
▶ Spray medium skillet with cooking spray and heat over medium-high heat 1 minute. Add chops in 2 batches and cook 10 minutes or until browned. Set chops aside.
▶ Remove pan from heat. Spray with cooking spray. Reduce heat to medium. Add onion and cook until tender-crisp.
▶ Stir cornstarch mixture and add. Cook until mixture boils and thickens, stirring constantly. Return chops to pan. Reduce heat to low. Cover and cook 5 minutes or until chops are no longer pink. Serve with noodles.

Serves 6 • Prep Time: 5 minutes • Cook Time: 35 minutes

Nutritional Values Per Serving: Calories 404, Total Fat 10g, Saturated Fat 3g, Cholesterol 121mg, Sodium 362mg, Total Carbohydrate 44g, Protein 32g

Pork need not be a forbidden food when planning low-fat meals. Choose lean cuts like bone-in or boneless pork loin chops. Use vegetable cooking spray as a browning aid instead of margarine or butter.

▲ Smothered Pork Chops

GLAZED PORK CHOPS WITH CORN STUFFING

1   can (14½ ounces) SWANSON NATURAL GOODNESS Chicken Broth
⅛   teaspoon ground red pepper
1   cup frozen whole kernel corn
1   stalk celery, chopped (about ½ cup)
1   medium onion, chopped (about ½ cup)
4   cups PEPPERIDGE FARM Corn Bread Stuffing
6   boneless pork chops, ¾ inch thick (about 1½ pounds)
2   tablespoons packed brown sugar
2   teaspoons spicy-brown mustard

▶ In saucepan mix broth, pepper, corn, celery and onion. Over medium-high heat, heat to a boil. Remove from heat. Add stuffing. Mix lightly.

▶ Spray 3-quart shallow baking dish with *vegetable cooking spray*. Spoon stuffing into dish. Arrange chops over stuffing. Mix sugar and mustard. Spread over chops. If desired, sprinkle *paprika* over chops.

▶ Bake at 400°F. for 30 minutes or until chops are no longer pink.

Serves 6 • Prep Time: 20 minutes • Cook Time: 30 minutes

Nutritional Values Per Serving: Calories 376, Total Fat 10g, Saturated Fat 3g, Cholesterol 67mg, Sodium 693mg, Total Carbohydrate 41g, Protein 29g

ONE-DISH BEEF STROGANOFF AND NOODLES

¾   pound boneless beef top round steak, ¾ inch thick
1   can (10¾ ounces) CAMPBELL'S HEALTHY REQUEST condensed
       Cream of Mushroom Soup
1   can (14½ ounces) SWANSON Beef Broth
½   cup water
1   medium onion, sliced (about ½ cup)
3   cups dry medium egg noodles
½   cup plain yogurt

▶ Slice beef into very thin strips.

▶ In medium nonstick skillet over medium-high heat, cook beef until browned, stirring often. Set beef aside.

▶ Add soup, broth, water and onion. Heat to a boil. Stir in noodles. Reduce heat to low. Cook 10 minutes or until noodles are done, stirring often. Stir in yogurt. Return beef to pan and heat through.

Serves 4 • Prep Time: 10 minutes • Cook Time: 25 minutes

Nutritional Values Per Serving: Calories 308, Total Fat 7g, Saturated Fat 2g, Cholesterol 87mg, Sodium 799mg, Total Carbohydrate 31g, Protein 29g

▲ Glazed Pork Chops with Corn Stuffing

FISH STEAKS DIJON

1 **can (14½ ounces) SWANSON Chicken Broth**
1 **tablespoon Dijon-style mustard**
1 **teaspoon lemon juice**
⅛ **teaspoon pepper**
1½ **pounds swordfish steaks, 1 inch thick**
1 **tablespoon cornstarch**

▶ Mix broth, mustard, lemon juice and pepper. Pour *1 cup* broth mixture into large shallow nonmetallic dish. Add fish and turn to coat. Cover and refrigerate 1 hour, turning fish occasionally.

▶ In small saucepan mix cornstarch and remaining broth mixture until smooth. Set aside.

▶ Remove fish from marinade and place on lightly oiled grill rack over medium-hot coals. Grill uncovered 10 minutes or until fish flakes easily when tested with a fork, turning once and brushing often with marinade. Discard marinade.

▶ Over medium heat, heat cornstarch mixture until mixture boils and thickens, stirring constantly. Serve with fish. If desired, garnish with *cracked pepper*.

Serves 6 • Prep Time: 5 minutes • Marinating Time: 1 hour
Cook Time: 10 minutes

Nutritional Values Per Serving: Calories 140, Total Fat 5g, Saturated Fat 1g, Cholesterol 41mg, Sodium 447mg, Total Carbohydrate 2g, Protein 21g

Broiled Fish Steaks Dijon: Prepare as in first and second steps. In third step, remove fish from marinade and place on rack in broiler pan. Broil 4 inches from heat 10 minutes or until fish flakes easily when tested with a fork, turning once and brushing often with marinade. Discard marinade. Proceed as in fourth step.

M*any popular varieties of fish are low in fat. When steeped in a tangy, moist marinade based on SWANSON Broth, fish doesn't need added fat to be delicious.*

▲ Fish Steaks Dijon

ROAST BEEF WITH GRAVY

3   pound beef eye of round roast
1   can (14½ ounces) SWANSON Beef Broth
3   tablespoons all-purpose flour

▶ Place beef in shallow roasting pan. Insert meat thermometer into meat. Roast at 350°F. for 18 minutes per pound or until thermometer reads 155°F. (medium). Set beef aside. Pour off fat.
▶ In roasting pan gradually mix broth into flour until smooth. Over medium heat, cook until mixture boils and thickens, stirring constantly. Serve with beef.

Serves 12 • Prep Time: 5 minutes • Cook Time: About 1 hour

Nutritional Values Per Serving: Calories 126, Total Fat 4g, Saturated Fat 1g, Cholesterol 47mg, Sodium 193mg, Total Carbohydrate 2g, Protein 20g

"SKINNY" MASHED POTATOES

1   can (14½ ounces) SWANSON Chicken Broth
    Generous dash pepper
1⅓ cups instant mashed potato flakes *or* buds

▶ In medium saucepan over medium-high heat, heat broth and pepper to a boil. Stir in potato flakes until liquid is absorbed.

Serves 4 • Prep Time: 5 minutes • Cook Time: 5 minutes

Nutritional Values Per Serving: Calories 64, Total Fat 1g, Saturated Fat 0g, Cholesterol 0mg, Sodium 456mg, Total Carbohydrate 13g, Protein 2g

Deglaze the roasting pan with SWANSON Broth for a rich-tasting beef gravy.

▲ Roast Beef with Gravy and "Skinny" Mashed Potatoes

HOME-STYLE BEEF STEW

1 pound beef for stew, cut into 1-inch cubes
1 can (14½ ounces) SWANSON Beef Broth
1 bay leaf
½ teaspoon dried thyme leaves, crushed
⅛ teaspoon pepper
3 medium carrots (about ½ pound), cut into 1-inch pieces
2 medium potatoes (about ½ pound), cut into quarters
2 tablespoons all-purpose flour
¼ cup water

▶ In nonstick Dutch oven* over medium-high heat, cook beef until browned, stirring often.

▶ Add broth, bay leaf, thyme and pepper. Heat to a boil. Reduce heat to low. Cover and cook 1½ hours.

▶ Add carrots and potatoes. Cover and cook 30 minutes more or until beef is fork-tender, stirring occasionally.

▶ In cup mix flour and water until smooth. Gradually add to broth mixture. Over medium heat, cook until mixture boils and thickens, stirring constantly. Discard bay leaf. If desired, garnish with *fresh thyme*.

Serves 4 • Prep Time: 10 minutes • Cook Time: 2¼ hours

Nutritional Values Per Serving: Calories 252, Total Fat 6g, Saturated Fat 2g, Cholesterol 74mg, Sodium 525mg, Total Carbohydrate 18g, Protein 31g

* If you do not have a nonstick Dutch oven, spray Dutch oven with vegetable cooking spray.

BASIL AND GARLIC POTATOES

11 medium potatoes (about 3½ pounds), thinly sliced
4 cloves garlic, minced
2 teaspoons dried basil leaves, crushed
¼ teaspoon pepper
1 can (14½ ounces) SWANSON Chicken Broth

▶ In 3-quart shallow baking dish layer *half* the potatoes, garlic, basil and pepper. Repeat layers. Pour broth over potato mixture.

▶ Bake at 350°F. for 1 hour or until potatoes are tender.

Serves 12 • Prep Time: 15 minutes • Cook Time: 1 hour

Nutritional Values Per Serving: Calories 110, Total Fat 0g, Saturated Fat 0g, Cholesterol 0mg, Sodium 155mg, Total Carbohydrate 24g, Protein 3g

▲ Home-Style Beef Stew

GUILT-FREE ALFREDO

1 can (14½ ounces) SWANSON Chicken Broth
¼ cup all-purpose flour
¼ teaspoon garlic powder *or* 2 cloves garlic, minced
¼ teaspoon pepper
⅓ cup plain yogurt
6 cups hot cooked cholesterol-free noodle-style pasta (6 cups dry),
    cooked without salt
6 tablespoons grated Parmesan cheese
  Chopped fresh parsley

▶ In medium saucepan gradually mix broth into flour, garlic powder and pepper until smooth. Over medium heat, cook until mixture boils and thickens, stirring constantly.

▶ Remove from heat. Stir in yogurt. Toss with pasta and *4 tablespoons* cheese. Sprinkle with parsley and remaining cheese. If desired, garnish with *carrot, lemon verbena* and *rose leaves*.

Serves 6 • Prep Time: 10 minutes • Cook Time: 15 minutes

Nutritional Values Per Serving: Calories 178, Total Fat 3g, Saturated Fat 1g, Cholesterol 5mg, Sodium 402mg, Total Carbohydrate 30g, Protein 9g

CREAMY CLAM CHOWDER

1 can (14½ ounces) SWANSON NATURAL GOODNESS Chicken Broth
¼ teaspoon dried thyme leaves, crushed
⅛ teaspoon pepper
3 medium potatoes, peeled and cut into cubes (about 3 cups)
1 stalk celery, sliced (about ½ cup)
1 medium onion, chopped (about ½ cup)
1½ cups milk
2 tablespoons all-purpose flour
2 cans (6½ ounces *each*) minced clams

▶ In medium saucepan mix broth, thyme, pepper, potatoes, celery and onion. Over high heat, heat to a boil. Reduce heat to low. Cover and cook 15 minutes or until vegetables are tender.

▶ In bowl gradually mix milk into flour until smooth. Gradually add to broth mixture. Add clams. Cook until mixture boils and thickens, stirring constantly.

Serves 7 • Prep Time: 15 minutes • Cook Time: 25 minutes

Nutritional Values Per Serving: Calories 137, Total Fat 2g, Saturated Fat 1g, Cholesterol 4mg, Sodium 561mg, Total Carbohydrate 20g, Protein 11g

▲ Guilt-Free Alfredo

CHICKEN PASTA SALAD

1 can (14½ ounces) SWANSON NATURAL GOODNESS Chicken Broth
½ cup plain yogurt
¼ cup grated Parmesan cheese
1 teaspoon dried dill weed *or* dried basil leaves, crushed
3 cups hot cooked corkscrew macaroni (about 2½ cups dry),
    cooked without salt
1 cup cherry tomatoes cut in half
1 cup frozen peas
½ cup sliced mushrooms (about 2 ounces)
1 small red onion, chopped (about ¼ cup)
2 cups cubed cooked chicken
  Lettuce leaves

▶ In medium bowl, with fork, mix broth, yogurt, cheese and dill weed.

▶ In large shallow nonmetallic dish toss macaroni, tomatoes, peas, mushrooms, onion, chicken and broth mixture until evenly coated. Refrigerate at least 4 hours or overnight, stirring occasionally. Serve on lettuce. If desired, garnish with *additional tomato*.

Serves 4 • Prep Time: 20 minutes • Chill Time: 4 hours

Nutritional Values Per Serving: Calories 373, Total Fat 8g, Saturated Fat 3g, Cholesterol 57mg, Sodium 678mg, Total Carbohydrate 42g, Protein 31g

HERBED VEGETABLE STUFFING

1 can (14½ ounces) SWANSON NATURAL GOODNESS Chicken Broth
  Generous dash pepper
1 stalk celery, coarsely chopped (about ½ cup)
½ cup sliced mushrooms (about 2 ounces)
1 small onion, coarsely chopped (about ¼ cup)
4 cups PEPPERIDGE FARM Herb Seasoned Stuffing

▶ In medium saucepan mix broth, pepper, celery, mushrooms and onion. Over medium-high heat, heat to a boil. Reduce heat to low. Cover and cook 5 minutes or until vegetables are tender. Remove from heat. Add stuffing. Mix lightly.

▶ Spoon into 1½-quart casserole. Bake at 350°F. for 20 minutes or until hot.

Serves 8 • Prep Time: 15 minutes • Cook Time: 20 minutes

Nutritional Values Per Serving: Calories 122, Total Fat 1g, Saturated Fat 0g, Cholesterol 0mg, Sodium 545mg, Total Carbohydrate 23g, Protein 4g

▲ Chicken Pasta Salad

VEGETABLE RICE PILAF

Vegetable cooking spray
¾ **cup uncooked regular long-grain rice**
1 **can (14½ ounces) SWANSON Vegetable Broth**
¼ **teaspoon dried basil leaves, crushed**
¾ **cup frozen mixed vegetables**
¼ **cup chopped red *or* green pepper**

▶ Spray medium saucepan with cooking spray and heat over medium heat 1 minute. Add rice and cook 30 seconds, stirring constantly. Stir in broth and basil. Heat to a boil. Reduce heat to low. Cover and cook 10 minutes.
▶ Stir in vegetables and pepper. Cover and cook 10 minutes more or until rice is done and most of liquid is absorbed. If desired, garnish with *fresh chives*.

Serves 4 • Prep Time: 5 minutes • Cook Time: 25 minutes

Nutritional Values Per Serving: Calories 171, Total Fat 1g, Saturated Fat 0g, Cholesterol 0mg, Sodium 459mg, Total Carbohydrate 37g, Protein 4g

CREAMY POTATO SOUP

1 **can (14½ ounces) SWANSON Chicken Broth**
⅛ **teaspoon pepper**
4 **green onions, sliced (about ½ cup)**
1 **stalk celery, sliced (about ½ cup)**
3 **medium potatoes (about 1 pound), peeled and sliced ¼ inch thick**
1½ **cups milk**

▶ In medium saucepan mix broth, pepper, onions, celery and potatoes. Over high heat, heat to a boil. Reduce heat to low. Cover and cook 15 minutes or until vegetables are tender. Remove from heat.
▶ In blender or food processor, place *half* the broth mixture and *¾ cup* milk. Cover and blend until smooth. Repeat with remaining broth mixture and remaining milk. Return to pan. Over medium heat, heat through.

Serves 5 • Prep Time: 15 minutes • Cook Time: 30 minutes

Nutritional Values Per Serving: Calories 121, Total Fat 2g, Saturated Fat 1g, Cholesterol 6mg, Sodium 406mg, Total Carbohydrate 21g, Protein 5g

▲ Vegetable Rice Pilaf

INTERNATIONAL
collection

▼

Here's a fabulous selection of ethnic recipes that are streamlined in preparation and in fat, too! You'll come to rely on recipes like scrumptious *Easy Chicken Paprikash,* a slimmed down version of Hungarian Goulash. *Beef and Broccoli* features a stir-fry technique you will use often in low-fat cooking — substituting SWANSON Broth for added fat. These great-tasting, easy recipes enable you to be an international cook any day of the week!

Easy Chicken Paprikash, left (page 81) and *Oriental Chicken and Vegetable Stir-Fry,* right (page 80).

ORIENTAL CHICKEN AND VEGETABLE STIR-FRY

2 tablespoons cornstarch
1 can (14½ ounces) SWANSON Oriental Broth
1 pound skinless, boneless chicken breasts, cut into strips
5 cups cut-up vegetables*
4 cups hot cooked rice, cooked without salt

▶ In bowl mix cornstarch and *1 cup* broth until smooth. Set aside.
▶ In medium nonstick skillet over medium-high heat, stir-fry chicken in 2 batches until browned. Set chicken aside.
▶ Add remaining broth and vegetables. Heat to a boil. Reduce heat to low. Cover and cook 5 minutes or until vegetables are tender-crisp.
▶ Stir cornstarch mixture and add. Cook until mixture boils and thickens, stirring constantly. Return chicken to pan and heat through. Serve over rice. If desired, garnish with *radishes* and *red pepper.*

Serves 4 • Prep Time: 15 minutes • Cook Time: 25 minutes

Nutritional Values Per Serving: Calories 452, Total Fat 4g, Saturated Fat 1g, Cholesterol 73mg, Sodium 634mg, Total Carbohydrate 68g, Protein 34g

*Use a combination of broccoli flowerets, green onions cut in 1-inch pieces, sliced celery and sliced carrot.

Y*ou can vary the vegetables in this recipe according to the season — mushrooms, red or green peppers and asparagus are just a few choices that would cook to perfection in this stir-fry.*

EASY CHICKEN PAPRIKASH

 4 skinless, boneless chicken breast halves (about 1 pound)
 1 can (14½ ounces) SWANSON Chicken Broth
 ¼ cup all-purpose flour
 2 teaspoons paprika
 ⅛ teaspoon ground red pepper
 1 medium onion, sliced (about ½ cup)
 ⅓ cup plain yogurt
 4 cups hot cooked wide egg noodles (about 4 cups dry),
      cooked without salt

▶ In medium nonstick skillet over medium-high heat, cook chicken 10 minutes or until browned. Set chicken aside.

▶ In same pan gradually mix broth into flour, paprika and pepper until smooth. Cook until mixture boils and thickens, stirring constantly. Return chicken to pan. Add onion. Reduce heat to low. Cover and cook 5 minutes or until chicken is no longer pink.

▶ Remove from heat. Stir in yogurt. Serve with noodles. If desired, garnish with *fresh parsley* and *tomato*.

Serves 4 • Prep Time: 10 minutes • Cook Time: 20 minutes

Nutritional Values Per Serving: Calories 415, Total Fat 7g, Saturated Fat 2g, Cholesterol 126mg, Sodium 529mg, Total Carbohydrate 50g, Protein 37g

From mild to fiery hot, the pungent Hungarian varieties of paprika are held in highest regard. In quantities used for flavoring, paprika contributes to the Daily Value for Vitamin A.

MEDITERRANEAN CHICKEN AND RICE BAKE

    1 can (14½ ounces) SWANSON Chicken Broth
    ¼ cup chopped fresh parsley
    ¼ cup sliced VLASIC *or* EARLY CALIFORNIA pitted Ripe Olives
    1 tablespoon lemon juice
    ½ teaspoon turmeric (optional)
    ¼ teaspoon pepper
    1 can (about 14½ ounces) stewed tomatoes
 1¼   cups uncooked regular long-grain rice
    6 skinless, boneless chicken breast halves (about 1½ pounds)
    ½ teaspoon garlic powder

▶ In 3-quart shallow baking dish mix broth, parsley, olives, lemon juice, turmeric, pepper, tomatoes and rice. Cover and bake at 375°F. for 20 minutes.

▶ Place chicken on mixture. Sprinkle garlic powder and *paprika* over chicken. Bake uncovered 30 minutes more or until chicken is no longer pink and rice is done. If desired, garnish with *fresh rosemary*.

Serves 6 • Prep Time: 10 minutes • Cook Time: 50 minutes

Nutritional Values Per Serving: Calories 326, Total Fat 5g, Saturated Fat 1g, Cholesterol 73mg, Sodium 635mg, Total Carbohydrate 38g, Protein 31g

LIGHT CHICKEN CACCIATORE

    4 skinless, boneless chicken breast halves (about 1 pound)
    1 can (14½ ounces) SWANSON Chicken Broth
    ½ teaspoon dried oregano leaves, crushed
    ½ teaspoon garlic powder
    1 can (14½ ounces) whole peeled tomatoes, cut up
    1 small green pepper, cut into 2-inch-long strips (about 1 cup)
    1 medium onion, cut into wedges
 2½   cups dry medium shell macaroni

▶ In medium nonstick skillet over medium-high heat, cook chicken 10 minutes or until browned. Set chicken aside.

▶ Add broth, oregano, garlic powder, tomatoes, pepper and onion. Heat to a boil. Stir in macaroni. Reduce heat to low. Cover and cook 10 minutes.

▶ Return chicken to pan. Cover and cook 5 minutes more or until chicken is no longer pink.

Serves 4 • Prep Time: 10 minutes • Cook Time: 30 minutes

Nutritional Values Per Serving: Calories 406, Total Fat 5g, Saturated Fat 1g, Cholesterol 73mg, Sodium 732mg, Total Carbohydrate 53g, Protein 36g

▲ Mediterranean Chicken and Rice Bake

GARLIC PORK KABOBS

2 tablespoons cornstarch
1 can (14½ ounces) SWANSON Oriental Broth
2 cloves garlic, minced
1 tablespoon *each* packed brown sugar *and* ketchup
2 teaspoons vinegar
1 pound boneless pork loin, cut into 1-inch cubes
12 medium mushrooms
1 large red onion, cut into 12 wedges
4 cherry tomatoes
4 cups hot cooked rice, cooked without salt

▶ In small saucepan mix cornstarch, broth, garlic, sugar, ketchup and vinegar until smooth. Over medium heat, cook until mixture boils and thickens, stirring constantly.

▶ On 4 long skewers, thread pork, mushrooms and onion alternately.

▶ Place kabobs on lightly oiled grill rack over medium-hot coals. Grill uncovered 20 minutes or until pork is no longer pink, turning and brushing often with broth mixture. Place one tomato on end of each skewer.

▶ Heat remaining broth mixture to a boil. Serve with kabobs and rice.

Serves 4 • Prep Time: 15 minutes • Cook Time: 25 minutes

Nutritional Values Per Serving: Calories 485, Total Fat 9g, Saturated Fat 3g, Cholesterol 68mg, Sodium 604mg, Total Carbohydrate 69g, Protein 31g

SPANISH BEEF AND RICE

¾ pound lean ground beef (85% lean)
1 large onion, chopped (about 1 cup)
1 medium green pepper, chopped (about ¾ cup)
1 can (14½ ounces) SWANSON Beef Broth
1 can (8 ounces) tomato sauce
1 tablespoon chili powder
½ teaspoon garlic powder
¾ cup uncooked regular long-grain rice

▶ In skillet over medium-high heat, cook beef, onion and pepper until beef is browned, stirring to separate meat. Pour off fat. Add broth, tomato sauce, chili powder and garlic. Heat to a boil. Stir in rice. Reduce heat to low. Cover and cook 20 minutes or until rice is done.

Serves 4 • Prep Time: 10 minutes • Cook Time: 30 minutes

Nutritional Values Per Serving: Calories 386, Total Fat 11g, Saturated Fat 4g, Cholesterol 59mg, Sodium 885mg, Total Carbohydrate 48g, Protein 23g

▲ Garlic Pork Kabobs

SZECHUAN SHRIMP

3 tablespoons cornstarch
1 can (14½ ounces) SWANSON Oriental Broth
½ teaspoon garlic powder
¼ teaspoon crushed red pepper
4 green onions, cut into 1-inch pieces (about 1 cup)
1 pound medium shrimp, shelled and deveined
4 cups hot cooked rice, cooked without salt

▶ In medium saucepan mix cornstarch, broth, garlic powder, pepper and onions. Over medium-high heat, cook until mixture boils and thickens, stirring constantly.
▶ Add shrimp. Cook 5 minutes or until shrimp turn pink, stirring often. Serve over rice.

Serves 4 • Prep Time: 15 minutes • Cook Time: 10 minutes

Nutritional Values Per Serving: Calories 359, Total Fat 2g, Saturated Fat 0g, Cholesterol 147mg, Sodium 669mg, Total Carbohydrate 62g, Protein 22g

BEEF AND BROCCOLI

1 pound boneless beef top round steak, ¾ inch thick
3 tablespoons cornstarch
1 can (14½ ounces) SWANSON Oriental Broth
1 tablespoon packed brown sugar
½ teaspoon garlic powder
4 cups broccoli flowerets
4 cups hot cooked rice, cooked without salt

▶ Slice beef into very thin strips. In bowl mix cornstarch, *1 cup* broth and sugar until smooth. Set aside.
▶ In medium nonstick skillet over medium-high heat, stir-fry beef in 2 batches until browned. Set beef aside.
▶ Add remaining broth, garlic powder and broccoli. Heat to a boil. Reduce heat to low. Cover and cook 5 minutes or until broccoli is tender-crisp.
▶ Stir cornstarch mixture and add. Cook until mixture boils and thickens, stirring constantly. Return beef to pan and heat through. Serve over rice.

Serves 4 • Prep Time: 15 minutes • Cook Time: 25 minutes

Nutritional Values Per Serving: Calories 480, Total Fat 6g, Saturated Fat 2g, Cholesterol 74mg, Sodium 576mg, Total Carbohydrate 68g, Protein 36g

▲ Szechuan Shrimp

FIESTA CHICKEN SOUP

Vegetable cooking spray
1 pound skinless, boneless chicken breasts, cut into cubes
1 large green *and/or* red pepper, coarsely chopped (about 1 cup)
2 teaspoons chili powder
1 teaspoon garlic powder
2 cans (14½ ounces *each*) SWANSON NATURAL GOODNESS
   Chicken Broth
1 package (10 ounces) frozen whole kernel corn (about 1¾ cups)
1 cup cooked rice, cooked without salt
1 teaspoon chopped fresh cilantro *or* parsley (optional)
5 lime wedges

▶ Spray large saucepan with cooking spray and heat over medium heat 1 minute. Add chicken, pepper, chili powder and garlic powder and cook 5 minutes, stirring often.

▶ Add broth, corn and rice. Heat to a boil. Reduce heat to low. Cook 10 minutes or until chicken is no longer pink. Stir in cilantro. Serve with lime wedges. If desired, garnish with additional *fresh cilantro.*

Serves 5 • Prep Time: 15 minutes • Cook Time: 20 minutes

Nutritional Values Per Serving: Calories 239, Total Fat 4g, Saturated Fat 1g, Cholesterol 58mg, Sodium 505mg, Total Carbohydrate 27g, Protein 26g

TORTELLINI SOUP

2 cans (14½ ounces *each*) SWANSON NATURAL GOODNESS
   Chicken Broth
⅛ teaspoon pepper
1 medium carrot, sliced (about ½ cup)
1 stalk celery, sliced (about ½ cup)
2 ounces frozen cheese-filled tortellini (about ½ cup)
1 tablespoon chopped fresh parsley *or* 1 teaspoon dried parsley flakes

▶ In medium saucepan mix broth, pepper, carrot and celery. Over medium-high heat, heat to a boil. Add tortellini. Reduce heat to medium. Cook 15 minutes or until tortellini is done, stirring occasionally. Stir in parsley.

Serves 4 • Prep Time: 10 minutes • Cook Time: 20 minutes

Nutritional Values Per Serving: Calories 79, Total Fat 2g, Saturated Fat 1g, Cholesterol 9mg, Sodium 656mg, Total Carbohydrate 10g, Protein 5g

▲ Fiesta Chicken Soup

MEXICAN BEANS AND RICE

1 **can (14½ ounces) SWANSON Chicken Broth**
½ **teaspoon ground cumin**
⅛ **teaspoon black pepper**
1 **medium onion, chopped (about ½ cup)**
1 **small green pepper, chopped (about ½ cup)**
¾ **cup uncooked regular long-grain rice**
1 **can (about 15 ounces) kidney beans, rinsed and drained**

▶ In medium saucepan mix broth, cumin, black pepper, onion and green pepper. Over medium-high heat, heat to a boil. Stir in rice. Reduce heat to low. Cover and cook 20 minutes or until rice is done and most of liquid is absorbed.
▶ Add beans and heat through. If desired, garnish with *lime, fresh cilantro* and *sweet red pepper.*

Serves 5 • Prep Time: 10 minutes • Cook Time: 30 minutes

Nutritional Values Per Serving: Calories 227, Total Fat 1g, Saturated Fat 0g, Cholesterol 0mg, Sodium 558mg, Total Carbohydrate 44g, Protein 10g

GERMAN POTATO SALAD

10 **medium potatoes (about 3 pounds)**
1 **can (14½ ounces) SWANSON Beef Broth**
¼ **cup all-purpose flour**
3 **tablespoons sugar**
½ **teaspoon celery seed**
½ **teaspoon salt**
⅛ **teaspoon pepper**
¼ **cup cider vinegar**
1 **medium onion, chopped (about ½ cup)**
3 **tablespoons chopped fresh parsley**

▶ In Dutch oven place potatoes. Cover with water. Over high heat, heat to a boil. Cook 20 minutes or until tender. Drain. Cut into cubes.
▶ In medium saucepan gradually mix broth into flour, sugar, celery seed, salt and pepper until smooth. Add vinegar and onion. Over medium heat, cook until mixture boils and thickens, stirring constantly. Reduce heat to low. Cook 5 minutes or until onion is tender.
▶ In large bowl toss potatoes, parsley and broth mixture until evenly coated.

Serves 12 • Prep Time: 15 minutes • Cook Time: 20 minutes

Nutritional Values Per Serving: Calories 158, Total Fat 0g, Saturated Fat 0g, Cholesterol 0mg, Sodium 336mg, Total Carbohydrate 35g, Protein 4g

▲ Mexican Beans and Rice

RECIPE INDEX

RECIPE INDEX

RECIPE INDEX

RECIPE BY PRODUCT INDEX

SENSIBLY DELICIOUS HINTS FROM SWANSON BROTH

Low-Fat Cooking Tips

▶ Use SWANSON Broth as a quick, low-fat base for sauces and gravies (see Orange-Glazed Chicken, page 18).

▶ For plenty of added flavor but no added fat*, marinate poultry, vegetables and fish in SWANSON Broth (see Marinated Turkey Breast, page 22).

▶ Toss cooked pasta with some SWANSON Broth instead of oil to prevent it from sticking together.

▶ For a delicious low-fat stuffing with lots of flavor, substitute SWANSON Broth for margarine or butter (see Apple Raisin Stuffing, page 42).

▶ When making gravy, reduce the amount of drippings to 1 tablespoon. Use 1 can (14½ ounces) SWANSON Broth plus 3 tablespoons flour.

▶ Use SWANSON Broth for "stir-frying" instead of oil.

▶ For added flavor, use SWANSON Broth instead of water when simmering vegetables, poaching fish or chicken (see Poached Fish Fillets, page 34).

▶ Use vegetable cooking sprays when a recipe calls for a greased pan or baking dish.

▶ Replace butter and milk in mashed potatoes with SWANSON Chicken or Vegetable Broth (see "Skinny" Mashed Potatoes, page 68).

Sensible Low-Fat Snacking

▶ A cup of hot SWANSON Broth
▶ Plain popcorn, without butter or oil
▶ Non-fat cottage cheese
▶ Unsalted pretzels
▶ Non-fat yogurt

▶ Unsweetened fruit juice
▶ Fruit slices with peels (for more fiber)
▶ Tomato or "V8" vegetable juice
▶ Cut-up raw vegetables
▶ Reduced-fat cookies or crackers

* Swanson Broths are at least 99% fat free.